ANIMALS WITHOUT BRAINS!

CORALS ARE BRAINLESS!

By Amanda Vink

Gareth Stevens Publishing

Please visit our website, www.garethstevens.com. For a free color catalog of all our high-quality books, call toll free 1-800-542-2595 or fax 1-877-542-2596.

Library of Congress Cataloging-in-Publication Data
Names: Vink, Amanda, author.
Title: Corals are brainless! / Amanda Vink.
Description: New York : Gareth Stevens Publishing, [2020] | Series: Animals without brains | Includes index.
Identifiers: LCCN 2019013883| ISBN 9781538245781 (paperback) | ISBN 9781538245804 (library bound) | ISBN 9781538245798 (6 pack)
Subjects: LCSH: Corals–Juvenile literature.
Classification: LCC QL377.C5 V68 2020 | DDC 593.6–dc23
LC record available at https://lccn.loc.gov/2019013883

Published in 2020 by
Gareth Stevens Publishing
111 East 14th Street, Suite 349
New York, NY 10003

Designer: Sarah Liddell
Editor: Amanda Vink

Photo credits: Cover, p. 1 Richard Whitcombe/Shutterstock.com; background used throughout Sanjatosic/Shutterstock.com; p. 5 Pete Niesen/Shutterstock.com; p. 7 nicolasvoisin44/Shutterstock.com; p. 9 SARAWUT KUNDEJ/Shutterstock.com; p. 11 Gerald Robert Fischer/Shutterstock.com; p. 13 Off Axis Production/Shutterstock.com; p. 15 (hard coral) littlesam/Shutterstock.com; p. 15 (soft coral) Cigdem Sean Cooper/Shutterstock.com; p. 17 Vlad61/Shutterstock.com; p. 19 Wild Horizon/Contributor/Universal Images Group/Getty Images; p. 21 Dudarev Mikhail/Shutterstock.com.

Printed in the United States of America

CPSIA compliance information: Batch #CW20GS: For further information contact Gareth Stevens, New York, New York at 1-800-542-2595.

CONTENTS

Boldface words appear in the glossary.

Brainless!

Corals are a group of small animals that come in many shapes. Though some look like human brains, corals are actually brainless! Corals have a simple **nervous system**, which sends messages around the body very differently than in a human.

Invertebrates

Corals don't have a backbone, or the column of bones that protects the spinal cord. Animals without backbones and bony **skeletons** are called invertebrates. Invertebrates make up about 97 percent of the animal kingdom.

Plant Vs. Animal

Some corals look like colorful plants or rocks. A coral sticks itself to the bottom of the ocean floor and grows upward. But corals are actually animals! Like other animals, they cannot make their own food. But unlike most other animals, corals don't have brains.

Nerve Net

How do corals live without a brain? A coral's simple nervous system is called a nerve net. Nerves are a type of cell that carry messages throughout the body. In humans, these messages are sent to and from the brain.

STONY CORAL

A Response

A coral's nerves are spread across its body. They pick up changes in light and movement around the coral. The coral responds, or reacts, to the messages received through its nerve net. For example, it might move toward light.

Polyps

The living part of a coral is called a polyp. Polyps have soft bodies with mouths circled by **tentacles**. Hard coral polyps use a **mineral** called calcium to build structures around themselves for safety. Soft corals look like colorful plants.

HARD CORAL

SOFT CORAL

Coral Reefs

Corals build important coral reefs. They are a place where many animals live. In fact, coral reefs are home to some of the most **diverse** life on Earth! They also keep **coastlines** from eroding, or wearing away.

Food

Polyps have stinging cells on their tentacles, which they use to pull tiny organisms called **plankton** into their mouths. Coral provides **algae** with a place to live, and in exchange the algae gives coral some of the food it makes. Algae makes coral colorful!

Coral Smarts

Corals live in **colonies**. They are found in salt water and need sun to live. People have to be careful not to harm corals. They may be brainless, but they are an important part of our planet!

GLOSSARY

algae: plantlike living things that are mostly found in water

coastline: the land along the edge of a coast

colony: a group of animals living and working together

diverse: differing from each other

mineral: matter in the ground that forms rocks

nervous system: the system of nerves in the body that sends messages for controlling movement and feeling

plankton: a tiny plant or animal that floats in the ocean

skeleton: the bony frame of the body

tentacle: a long, thin body part that sticks out from an animal's head or mouth

FOR MORE INFORMATION

BOOKS

Baby Professor. *Coral Reefs: A Whole New World Under the Sea – Nature Encyclopedia for Kids*. Newark, DE: Speedy Publishing LLC, 2017.

Rattini, Kristin. *National Geographic Readers: Coral Reefs.* Washington, DC: National Geographic Society, 2015.

WEBSITES

Kids Discover: "Brainless in the Animal Kingdom"
www.kidsdiscover.com/teacherresources/brainless-animal-kingdom/
Check out this blog post and website to learn more about brainless species and invertebrates in the animal kingdom.

World Biomes: Coral Reef
kids.nceas.ucsb.edu/biomes/coralreef.html
Dive into the world of ecology with this website, which offers more information and games about coral reefs.

Publisher's note to educators and parents: Our editors have carefully reviewed these websites to ensure that they are suitable for students. Many websites change frequently, however, and we cannot guarantee that a site's future contents will continue to meet our high standards of quality and educational value. Be advised that students should be closely supervised whenever they access the internet.

INDEX